The Fall and The Rise of a Black Man in Love

D'Marcus T. Glasper

Front cover design illustrated by Andre' Foster.

BROWN ESSENCE, INC.
P.O. BOX 82462
CONYERS, GA 30013

Please visit our website at brownessence.com and let us know what you think.

I write the duality that is humanity for without darkness we could not know light.

- D'Marcus T. Glasper

This book is dedicated to the true loves of my life... My mother Shon,
My grandmother Dora,
and my little sister Treazure...

TABLE OF CONTENTS

THE FALL

THE RISE

THE DEDICATION

This is the Dedication,
I dedicate this to those who seek LIBERATION
From their everyday lives,
For anyone who has ever searched for love
But didn't have THE DEFINITION,
For any woman that has ever been
the victim of BAD INTENTIONS,
For any man that has been caught up in
ENCHANTMENT by any girl,
But just felt INSUFFICIENT,
For anyone who has given up peace of MIND,
I've given a PIECE OF mine,
For the lovers who've given their
ALL FOR NOTHING,
Just because they wasted their time away
For one who was Under Construction,
This is for every EXCEPTIONAL woman
        that hasn't forgotten
The art of MENTAL SEDUCTION,
This is for anyone who has ever been BROKEN
Because someone tried to SELL YOU A DREAM,
I hope that you find peace,
Let me reiterate to you
That I dedicate this to everyone out there,

And I pray that every WANDERER
seeking love finds a love,
And anyone that love finds,
I hope you find time to remember CARPE DIEM,
Grab life by the horns
And never be afraid of the thorns of love,
Whether you're plain Jane,
Or Lois Lane to a SUPER MAN,
But mostly I hope you all FALL FOR ME
And ASK ME TO STAY,
Because there is nowhere in the world
that I would rather be,
Than here sharing my love with you

THE FALL, THE RISE

A life of perfect duality,
Living in a world of fantasy,
Always in the spotlight
But stuck in the darkness,
With no love in his heart
But a lot of love in his bedroom,
Right under all of the lights,
Living the awesomest life,
But torn apart inside
By the lies that he'd spread
And the hearts that he'd broken,
The path that he'd chosen
Was of the loneliest variety,
But his pride made him live for the glory,
Every woman nothing more than a trophy,
But pride always comes before the fall,
And when the flyest of them all
Comes crashing down,
He's never stopped by the ground,
Instead, he's plunged into the depths of sorrow,
Engulfed in a world of darkness,
And must learn to seek the light,
So come along on his road to redemption
As he attempts to conquer the Fall,
And ascend.

THE LIFE

BAD INTENTIONS

Nothing is as sweet as whispering sweet nothings
To the unsuspecting prey,
Emotionally unprotected,
They let me in so easily,
Throwing caution and inhibitions to the wind,
And I wind up with full control,
Give me domain,
Give me your brain
As I love them and leave them,
Desire and Flame,
Passion and pain,
Making them fall in love and acting the same,
They will never recognize my game,
And if they ever do they'll be in too deep,
Minds bent too far,
Forgotten who you are,
Because your thoughts are shrouded in the mist,
All because I call you "Miss"
Instead of this and that and all the above,
You thought you were in love,
And I suppose it's better than all the different

colored bones you were,
Yellow, Black, Brown, and Red,
So when I call you a lady it goes to your head,
But I'm just thinking with my head
Trying to see if we can head to my room
And let you see my headboard,
Until I'm bored with you,
Kiss you and dismiss you,
Forget who you thought I was,
I'm not a villain,
Just a man with bad intentions.

SELL YOU A DREAM

Under the guise of a lover,
It was easy to go under cover
And investigate the scene
That was your body,
And it may have been wrong
But it's been so long
Since I've met someone like you,
So I'll look you in the eyes,
And sell you a dream
Without telling you lies
So this opportunity doesn't slip through my fingers,
As I make sure this impression lingers
Upon your mind
Just like it's your first time,
And I'll make you fall, Love
So that you never leave,
Fall for me,
Don't be afraid,
For if I'm not there to catch you
There's a net below,
But forget those emotions,
Because at this moment we're all alone,
So for now I just want to
Kiss all of your erogenous zones
As I listen to your erotic moans,

As you whisper you love me
And ask that I never leave,
I tell you I won't
Though I know that we'll never be,
But since it benefits me,
I will continue to sell you a dream.

MENTAL SEDUCTION

I just want you to come over

And we can get a little closer,
But I'm not trying to be slick,
        girl I'm just wanting to hold you,
Maybe we can watch a movie
I'll even fix you a bite,
        just tell me what you like.
You can leave once we're through,
Or I could spend the night just holding you.

At the moment the sex is unimportant,
        and yes your body's amazing,
                but darling your mind is gorgeous...
And I would love to dig deeper,
        bring you to your intellectual climax,
No funny business,
Just trying to see where your mind is at,
And when you ask me do I mind rewinding that,
Is a reminder that the gentlemen
        are becoming extinct,
That chivalry is on the brink of destruction,
That we've lost the art of mental seduction,
Abstract cerebral eruptions reduced to
        almost nothing,

Imagination rendered useless because
everything is so blatant,
And nothing on Earth is sacred anymore.
So take it how you want
But unless you can seduce my mind
You can take it to the door,
I can take you to a show a little later
Because it's in my nature,
But face it, You'll be quickly replaced
If your mentality is common place,
I need a woman that is less impressed
By my car than by my drive,
That's what drives me,
Drives me crazy,
I learned a long time ago
That it's hard not to waste time
No matter how many times you've played this game,
To lead with the body rather than the mind
Is to have a nice watch that tells no time,
But if you seduce the brain
Everything else falls in line.
So without dancing, entrance me,
Hands free, Verbally,
Seduce me.

FALL FOR ME

If it means that I can be the only one,
Then you should fall,
Fall without fear of disappointment,
Fall without reservation,
Fall in the summer
Without a wonder
If I'll be there for the fall,
See I just want it all from you,
But you're afraid to give it up,
Because you remember when you used to
Fall for those other guys,
Fall for their lies and deceit,
Fall for the look in their eyes
When they told you it was real,
I promise I know how you feel
Because falling has such a negative connotation,
As you're sent on a descent toward the pavement
You fear that no one will catch you
And that you'll feel the pain of rock bottom,
But if you just
FALL for ME,
I've got you covered,
I'll love you 365 and 366 in a leap year
If you take that leap of faith,
And leap into my arms,

Because if you give me your all
I will give you the world,
So like the rain in the summer sky
Would you fall for me,
Like the river cascading off of a cliff
Would you fall for me,
Like a magician's audience
With ooh's and ah's of amazement
At just a simple illusion,
Would you
Fall for me?

BLAST FROM THE PAST

As I gaze upon a familiar face
I see her glance,
Beautiful was the way the light danced
In her eyes, As I'm approaching
I'm noticing that she's scoping me,
I'm walking towards her and stumble,
Hopefully, I can regain my composure,
I mosey on over, ask her if I know her,
Apparently she's a joker,
Playfully asked if I'm sober,
Then she reveals
that she indeed knew me in another time,
She starts to walk away,
I'm following close behind,
Trying to press rewind and
Scan the catalogs of my mind
To see where she may have held a role,
I told her I didn't see how I could
Misplace a face so beautiful
Even in the crowded hallways of my brain,
Then she called out a name,
A name that stirred emotions I had forgotten I knew,
The flashbacks she inspired of the
Events that had transpired
Ignited my mind and set my soul on fire,

The passion was at its peak
and every time I would kiss her on the cheek
or even speak it would make her weak,
I used to love her like an expert,
Then I cut her out like an excerpt,
And the feeling hit her so hard it made
her chest hurt,
That's the way it goes when dealing with
love, pain, and sex,
My brothers taught me:
how to play love games the best,
She snapped me back to reality,
Right then, I remembered who she was
She was my love's best friend,
She said, "See, to you this is all a game,
You make these girls fall in love and
barely remember names
when you're through with them,
This is how you ruin them,
And you can't tell me that you don't see it
Because I can tell you're intuitive,
So why do you play us?"
I stood speechless thinking of reasons
No genius could comprehend it
And no philosopher could find the meaning,
I closed my eyes and took a breath,
And by the time I opened them she had left,
And then I wondered

About all of the hearts I had ripped asunder
And under what influence my actions took place,
And at that moment,
Having to face the ghosts of long ago,
I hid my face, Changed my ways,
And hoped that Karma would not find me.

CARPE DIEM

When opportunity knocks,
how often do we really answer?
How many times can we just pass it
before it decides not to come back and,
Do they matter? By "they" I mean all the factors,
The inevitable facts of life that keep holding us back
Cuz, I don't think that opportunity really cares,
once it knocks then it's there,
Once it's gone then it's likely that
it's visits will be rare,
Maybe it's because you're scared, but beware,
Because all the things you fear are the things that
keep you from getting anywhere,
Open up the door and rest assured that if you don't
you may miss out on something more,
On what God has in store,
Pass it by, but watch out that girl or guy,
That you so longed for
might be just another passerby,
If u don't open up your eyes, and
Open up your heart,
Then you may not realize that they were just what
you were seeking from the start,
In life there's no restart, no resets or do-overs,
Just regrets and what-ifs, but not if you wanna,

Take chances, cuz life is a game of risks and rewards,
So live each day like your last,
cuz any day could be yours...

LOVE UNDEFINED

What is love when it's properly defined?
Is it something tangible or is it all inside the mind?
Is it all knowing or is it blind?
Or is it the tie that forever binds
two intertwined souls?
A catalyst when you spend time
you wonder where did time go,
Is it the gift inside that package
that you just signed for?
What is love?
Is it something you chase after or just let happen?
Is it something chemical or something magic?
Can you tell me if it's transient or everlasting?
Is it something that's endless or does it die
right along with the passion?
Is it perfect duality:
The ultimate combination of
positive and negative emotions,
That will have you going through the motions
When it's all bad just to get to the moments
When it's all good,
Hoping that it stays there forever,
Does it change like the weather?
Is it better than having all the riches known to man
Just to hold their hand?

Tell me,
What is Love?
Is it unconditional?
Because I must admit to you that I'm a bit cynical,
Does love have a limit or is it infinite?
Is it possible to love just a little bit?
Is it okay if we just love for the hell of it?
Is love a physical act or is it celibate,
What is love?
I guess I'll let you know when I locate it,
But I don't know if I'll look,
Love is complicated.

ENCHANTMENT

See I wanna just sit down wit her and just chill,

And I don't mean "chill" I mean, really just chill,
Just dig into her feelings,
Figure out if she feels me,
See if the guy she thinks she knows
reflects the real me,
Got me waiting, exercising patience,
Patiently observing,
It's like she's one of my patients,
Or experiments,
Whatever you wanna call it,
I don't know what to call you besides amazing,
How you take me on these journeys
through outer space
Just by the way you phrase things...
I don't know how you manage it,
Controlling a transient being such as I,
Attention forever fleeting,
Desire forever fleeing,
But you do it like you've done it all your life
or something,
A different type of woman,
Make me wanna write you something,
But you say you're not a fan of poetry,

I suppose if you don't like poems
I could write it down in prose,
You ignite my fire and with every day it grows,
Does it really matter if she doesn't decide to read it,
If it didn't I wouldn't pen it,
I could have called her but I chose to take the scenic
Route, and since I'm out and about
I just wanted to stop by and give you these flowers.
You do like flowers don't you?
They wilted in the heat,
But the thought's still just as sweet, ain't it?
Thinking too far ahead,
Maybe I'll take your name and change it,
My friends say that I'm insane and brainless
To try to play this the way I play this,
But this is not a game...
This could be something classic,
You can take it to the bank,
I'm gonna Chase what matters....
Life's full of gambles,
Reaching for love in the dark,
Hoping you grab the knife by the handle,
Because that's a long ambulance ride
But see my favorite past time,
The thing I do to pass time,
Is think of you, you're past fly,
Baby girl you're stellar...
Too far above all the rest,

To the moon, to the skies, to the stars with us love,
And oddly enough, that's all I've thought of all day
I may have just took it too far, too soon,
But I was running out of room
Up in my mind fully consumed
By you

CAT'S GOT MY TONGUE

I'm trying to find the words,
Searching for the letters,
That make up these words,
That make up this letter,
Don't know how to say it,
just gotta relieve some pressure,
Don't wanna scare ya,
Plus I don't wanna regret it,
Got confessions don't know how to express them
I'm trying to see,
Inhibitions, they just won't let me be
who I'm trying to be,
Can't say what I'm trying to say
But I'm feeling some kinda way,
Thinking, plotting, scheming,
contemplating every day,
I tried to tell you once,
But the conversation just went like, Umm..
I don't know how to say...
Well... what I mean is...
Every time I look at you I just see this...
I just... damn...
Can I... no...
If I... Maybe... I...
Then the call dropped,

Almost built the courage up to say it
then it all stopped,
Said that I would just tell you another time,
You called me back,
Asked me what I was sayin,
Just... Uh... Never mind,
Going with my better mind,
But never may there be a better time,
I'm running out of lines,
Hope I'm not outta line,
But I just know that if I got a chance
I don't want the next man to come
and get me outta mine,
So can I have some time,
But not too much,
Opportunity comes quick,
But I don't wanna rush,
But I want there to be an us,
Plus, I want to last a while,
I want to place on your face an eternal smile,
I would walk a thousand miles,
And jog right back here to stop those tears
And fix anything they left broken,
I kinda hope you get my drift,
Cuz I was tryna say it straight
But all I could say was this...

IF

If I looked you in the face
And I brought it to you straight,
I don't know if I could take it
If you turned and walked away
If I spoke what I was thinking,
Would you comprehend the meaning?
Would you really understand?
Or would you even believe it?
If I sat and told you the story,
Do you think that you'd adore me?
Would you think that I was truth?
Or think I did it for the glory?
But I figure if I never said it,
And kept wondering if
Then I know you'd never get it,
So rather than me regret it,
You just gon have to respect it...

STOP PLAYING

I told her that I loved her,
She told me to stop playing,
She told me that she knows about
all the games that men partake in
Just to break into a woman's thoughts,
And then convince them into taking
all their clothing off,
I scoffed at the thought,
And I tried to express to her
That those types of men were men
lesser than myself,
Completely ignoring the fact
That I had those same skeletons in my closet,
Totally appalled that she would take it there,
I decided to tell her off and make her aware
This was never about laying you down,
Which is why I'm staying around,
But I have no time for playing around
With emotions, as greatness is motioning
For me to move forward
So pardon my straightforwardness,
But I refuse to lose you
And have you be another "just another" to me,
Just an almost lover,
And all those times I almost walked out

Were because I almost loved you,
But I guess it's true that love knows not time,
And if we waited on the perfect time
We'd be waiting forever,
Attempting to get ready for love,
But love is like a river,
A continuous flow but forever changing,
So no two moments are ever the same,
And I guess what I'm saying is...
Well you know what the saying is,
Time waits for no man,
And I'm stuck waiting for you in no man's land,
Can't tell if I'm in the dead zone or the red zone,
Can't even get my head on straight,
Because all that I've given you Is all that I am
And all that you can tell me is to

Stop Playing.

BET THE FARM

In a flash it was gone,
With a bang it was destroyed,
Opportunity dissolving just as quickly as it appeared
Leaving an incredible void,
One day late and eight letters short,
But of course it was your choice not to say them,
Night after night she implored,
As she divulged how she adored you,
To match her,
to call when
she was about to go all in,
Too smart for your own good,
Played your cards in the best of ways,
Trying to read her poker face,
Trying not to overplay,
But didn't they tell you?
The house always wins.
If you would've just taken all your
chips and thrown em in,
Maybe you could've won,
But now you're sitting standing in the crowd,
Waiting on the one with the hot hand to slip,
Or just dip from the table,
Because before you go home for the night,
You gotta study your opponent before you bring

more chips to the table,
She played it perfect,
Sure she deserves it,
But you're about to bring
back your whole check
To play the odds because she's worth it,
Staring down the dealer,
Intense focus,
Reading all the tales
to make sure you don't miss
the moment.

THE FALL

FANTASTIC FAÇADE

Everything's so quiet now,
Not peaceful,
Just quiet,
Tension thicker than a video vixen,
Silence louder than a lynch mob,
And I know I said I hated arguments,
But since we don't fight no more
It seems like we're not worth fighting for,
Just four months ago
It was all good,
When we would be together
It was like time got sped up,
But then you got fed up,
And I got fed up,
And nothing mattered but convenience,
Because it was just easier to stay,
Though it might be better that we break,
We just go through the motions,
Though all the emotion is gone
We let the public believe that the love is still strong,
But we don't even love no more
Just get our fixes
And go back to how it was before,
Just a silent separation Under the same roof,
Living a fantastic façade

WHEN THE FIRE DIES

Some wish for one kiss to make their heart flutter. Couples face much trouble puttin' up with one another. For lovers to be unhappy is more than the lonely can fathom. If only the lonely could imagine, because one day you live happily and the next is a tragedy, and you're at each other's necks and the sex ain't as passionate, and yet somehow you still fight the feelin.

The same feelin that's revealing that the feelin, just ain't real anymore, and you drop to your knees on the bedroom floor; ready to beat down heaven's door. Just for a love that you prayin doesn't diminish.

Prayin you reach the finish and prayin the love is endless. Break up and you come back. Walk away and you run back. Tryin everything under the sun to get the fun back, and you ain't just goin through the motions but it feels like the emotion is rare. All you can do is hope it's still there, and hope they still care, cuz there's a notion that the potion ain't there.

You just end up hopin that somethin can give you hope again. There ain't no openings and the walls are closin in. You wanna murder yo woman, you wanna choke yo man, but if it's meant to be then everything will fall in place, and fallin out of love is as painful as the fall from grace. So to the

lonely just be grateful but know love is amazing,
As long as you can keep the fire blazing...

ASK ME TO STAY

I'm trying to talk it out with you,
But you'll never listen,
You don't want to or you're too busy,
It's like every day I pray for something new,
A breakthrough for me and you,
But I know it's not comin,
Cuz though you should stand and fight,
You're runnin!
Hoping it never catches up,
I stand at the door about to leave
My bags, I've packed them up
And I told you that I've had enough,
I stand and I wait for you to ask me to stay,
But it doesn't matter if I go, does it,
I'll just charge it to the game,
Hope you owe nothing,
Cuz that's a hefty price to pay!
When karma makes her rounds
I hope she passes you,
It's scary how now when I pass
I can't even glance at you,
A true romantic I was,
Showed love when it wasn't deserved,
Friends called it absurd,
I called it true,

Love, I called it you,
Placed you above myself,
Cuz even when I didn't have it,
I made sure you did,
Promises never broken,
you showed me love,
Unspoken and unrefined,
All in due time, All my new rhymes
Came from situations that I was facing wit you,
Cuz I hated where I was
AND the places that you were taking me to,
But all in all you made me a better person,
I thank you for it,
Hopefully I won't become a bitter man
And hate you for it,
I know I said that we could just be friends,
But I can't ignore it,
So maybe this should just be the end,
What do you think?

ALL FOR NOTHING

Reduced to an empty shell,
An oyster with no pearl,
In love with the wrong girl,
Mad at the whole world,
I know how crazy it seems,
But I'm straining to breathe,
Without my lady, Maybe it's me,
But I feel like God is playing with me,
Holdin the prize right in front of me - to rip it away,
Just close enough for me to grip it
as I'm slippin away,
And as I fall I scream her name
hoping she catches me,
But she just waves goodbye as I fall,
witness the tragedy,
I was told she wrong for me
by friends and foes alike,
I would tell em I don't believe,
for me it just feels right,
And I'ma get shawty to be wit me hate it or love it,
But then I had no luck wit makin the lady love me,
And now I just feel empty cuz
I gave my heart away to this woman,
I love her more than I wanna,
I feel like hatin this woman,

I'm just a shell of a man, maybe I'm dumb,
Because I took my all and traded it all for nothin

AFRAID TO MOVE

I always knew that "love" did exist, but true love to me was always a myth. So I've always stood in the crossway of bliss and misery, afraid to move from here. And you came along and you grabbed my heart, And ran away, making me start To follow you, taking this car out of park, Now I'm ready to move from here. So I followed your path and it led me to love. The happiness here was more than enough. Loving with love that's more than a love. Never wanting to leave from here. Then I realized my horrendous blunder, You did not guide, Just aimlessly wandered, And your roads are not the same, I wonder Where in your world is here. You make my world begin to shift, The crossway of misery and bliss, That had for moments ceased to exist Came back and now still I'm here. My love was true, as you loved not, You made me strong enough to stop My fear, You took me high and dropped Me, and I landed back here. And I wait and wait for your return, I think about the lesson learned, The roads around me I'm concerned, Can never lead me there. To the place that you took me and left me alone, And then you left me and made it known, Misery would always be part of my home, And I cannot leave from here. For you cannot have bliss without the other, But one thing that I have discovered, Is that it doesn't work the other Way 'round, and I am there. There in the place where bliss doesn't accompany Misery, So instead of me suffering, I just decided that once was enough for me, And I'm never to leave from here. So if you must know, my only fear Is to leave from the nothingness that is here.

PIECE OF MIND

If I didn't say anything that would offend somebody,
I'd never say anything.

I'd never be able to say I love you
Because past flames would go insane
With thoughts of me moving on.

But at least I'd never say anything stupid,
Never say anything to hurt you,
Never have to apologize
For words I never should have said.

Tact has never been my forte
So, it's hard to hold words,
And often times I end up saying the wrong words,
I'll say the right subject, But say the wrong verb,
And try to catch myself before I say the whole word.

And what if my mind holds words that can change the whole world,
To never speak them would be a sin,
But then again I've brought great destruction with my tongue,
Along with great pleasure,
My words have killed and given life,
But maybe I should have never.

I've said what's on my mind,
I find it hard to tell a lot of lies,
But truth hurts a lot of times
And for that I apologize,
But I refuse to throw my truthfulness aside
Just because it might hurt your pride
I can't keep it bottled up inside.

I stand firm by every statement that I'm making,
No matter how blunt, No matter how brazen,
No matter how boring, No matter how amazing
Thoughts move at too great a pace, who am I to stop greatness?
I'm sorry that I can't please you with every word I speak,
I'm sorry if I offend, but it's fine if you disagree,
I'm sorry that the corruption is something you have to see,
I'm sorry that all I ever learned how to be is me.

THE WANDERER

He was showing all the signs
Of a man walking blind
Down a path all alone
Loneliness playing tricks with his mind,
He saw a girl standing on the side,
It wasn't the first one he saw,
Just the first that caught his eye,
He approached her,
Calm and so cultured,
You could never tell he was lonely
By the confidence he boasted,
His words enticed her,
As she wondered why he was all alone,
She listened in silence and waited
On this stranger to invite her
Into the parts of his heart
That held his inner thoughts,
She didn't know how tight he guarded them,
That's just how he was taught,
Because trust is hard to come by,
Easy to lose,
And the world taught him
Once you got 'em
They're so easy to use,
So he walked alone keeping people at a distance

And even when he spoke
It was with a certain indifference,
But this woman was different,
Or was she,
We just met but I still get the feeling
that you love me,
Will you walk with me?
Talk with me,
Take a stroll down this lonely road,
Be a companion for my lonely soul,
As they moseyed along
He walked a couple steps behind,
Because "too good to be true"
kept ringing in his mind,
So she asked him, come walk next to me,
You just met me, but I think this might be destiny,
He paused for a moment to question it,
Could it be, that word gets tossed around so loosely
She's just trying to use me,
I think that I'll play it cool,
I don't want to be stupid,
I've already played the fool,
I don't want to be foolish,
So he told her keep walking
He would catch up,
And when she slowed her pace
He backed up,
Afraid of his own heart

Because of what his brain told him,
It's just a different beat
But it's the same old hymn,
That he was a little more grown
But still the same old him,
But he was hoping he could change
And she would wait on him,
And then his heart started playing a song
It said anywhere she was
Felt like home,
He started sprinting up the road behind her,
Trying so hard to find her,
Caught her walking with someone else beside her,
She said she didn't see him coming,
By the time he started running
She was gone,
But when he found her
She said that she still loved him,
So he kept walking behind a couple steps,
Still alone, but walking strong
Because he knew he had next,
How wrong he was,
He thought is this love,
Because if it is, love,
It's a lonely love,
Or maybe it's only
An "Oh yeah, that's my homie" love,
She would occasionally slow down

To let him know she felt the same,
But he wasn't sure,
He felt like it was just a game,
He was going insane,
But the road was becoming more populated,
So he found another stranger
Thinking he could replace her,
But that would never happen,
Not even close,
He reverted to his old self,
He'd entertain them
But then he was getting ghost,
He kept in touch with her,
But thinking of someone else touching her
Was way too much to bear,
So as he expressed his love for her,
She slowly shed a tear,
And said I wish that you were here
But for now you're not
And I fear that for now you've lost your spot,
But he said he wouldn't give up,
He would sustain what he felt,
But his mind interjected,
And said, "Dude don't hold your breath,"
So will he persevere, will he endure it,
I guess we'll all see when we continue the story...

To Be Continued

HI, MY NAME IS SUPERMAN

I was endowed with incredible strength,
The strength to pull you through whatever
situation you encountered, and I had the power
To make my enemies cower in fear,
Not only that, but I possessed the strength
To carry any burden I was given,
So I put all those who needed me on my shoulders,
And I strolled on, with no sign of struggle.
I was also blessed with incredible speed,
To quickly maneuver in and out of a predicament,
So my movements away from pain were swift,
And my movements toward pleasure were swifter,
Speeding away from heartbreak,
Zooming into a new place of healing
That takes a regular human time to find.
And of course, I've got my X-ray vision,
With the capacity to see straight through you,
To look through those eyes and glare into your soul,
To look through your chest and read the words
flowing from your heart,
To look through the fake smiles of so called friends
And see their envy and their maliciousness,
To look through the happy mask you wear
and see your pain......................................
They said I was unstoppable,

They said I was unbeatable,
They said I had no flaws,
No weaknesses,
They said Achilles and Hercules
were only my prototypes,
So as far as they were concerned,
When I screamed, "Me against the world!"
They knew the world would lose.
They told me what doesn't kill you
Only makes you stronger,
And my whole life I've stared death in the face
Only to conquer time and time again,
An Invincible, Unbreakable, Immovable Force,
I would fly in and sweep you off your feet
And take you on a ride so thrilling that
Father Time had to stop his watch
Just to stop and watch.
And life was sweet,
I was too strong for mountains,
Flew too high for Valleys,
And when my world would begin to fall
And the foundations would crack and crumble,
I would hold up life with one hand and
fix the flaws with the other.
I was the one my friends looked to for strength,
Because they felt I was stronger,
I was the one that enemies could only glare at,
Because they knew the pinnacle of my success,

They knew I was unstoppable
And that no matter how they tried
They could not change the inevitable.
And though I sat with the world in my palm,
Never could I completely embrace my power,
Because in the back of my mind
I strived for normality,
A goal that was seemingly unattainable
To the likes of a Superman,
And I witnessed the stares of admiration
Transform into glares of envy,
Because I was better,
Never admitting it, and never flaunting it.
Of course there were those who still adored me,
The females who pined over me,
The guys who wanted to be just like me,
And the question arose,
The question that would forever alter my life
And the world's view of Superman,
Does Superman not long for a super woman?
As the universe hides its secrets,
I hid the tales of the loves I had encountered,
The "super" women that had graced my presence,
Each of them queens in their own right,
Each of them showing undying love for Superman,
Each of them with the capacity to lift me higher,
None of them with the ability to bring me down,
And in their disability to hurt me

Laid their greatest flaw.
In my search for normalcy,
I desperately needed a woman,
One who not only had the power to help me ascend,
But one with the power to send me
On a fiery, spiraling descent
So that I might crash to the ground
And understand true hurt
To appreciate true happiness.
Amazingly enough, on this quest for a woman
With power much greater than my own,
A woman by the name of Lois Lane came along,
And her voice sang a song sweeter
Than any I had heard from the many instruments
Of this vast planet, a voice to make
songbirds go mute,
Astonishingly, she was only human,
As frail as could be with a hurt in her eyes
That drew the hero in me
To fly to her rescue.
And as I stopped to hear her story,
I began to feel weaker,
And I, fearing a display of weakness,
Battled the tears in the back of my eyes,
And let them flow at the forefront of my soul,
And as I looked into her heart I saw something,
Something I had never before seen,
A stone glowing a passionate red,

That I named Kryptonite.
As I gazed upon this precious stone,
I realized that this must be
The source of this weakness I felt,
I longed for that stone,
And as a result longed for the heart of Lois Lane,
For in her heart was the one object
That could destroy Superman.
I began to spend every waking moment
Watching over and protecting her,
Saving her from all the world's ills,
And simultaneously fighting
For the acquisition of her heart,
But the more I was around
Miss Lane and this "Kryptonite",
The weaker I became.
An incredible pain would course through
The very fabric of my being,
Slowly destroying me with every failed attempt,
My X-ray vision clouded,
My strength hampered,
My speed rendered useless by insecurities
And a heavy heart that weighed me down,
And as tragic as it may seem,
I loved this feeling.
I loved to feel like I fit in,
Loved to feel human,
Loved to be no more than Clark Kent,

Until that fateful winter's morning,
When I woke up and understood
That I could never possess this Kryptonite
Nor the heart in which it was so securely encased.
An obsession was brewing,
A frantic feeling inside of me,
A raging fire that was consuming me,
And everything that was me,
Slowly burning away my sense of right and wrong,
Quickly scorching my will to truly live,
Death was not an option,
But life became a mere formality,
For only Kryptonite held the power,
The power to hurt me,
The power to destroy me.
If there was no way for me
To obtain and to control Kryptonite,
Then it was imperative that I avoided it
At any and all costs,
And I tried to shun Lois Lane,
Tried to hate her for making me feel this way,
Stood on the brink of destroying the one she loved,
Tried to ban her from my presence,
But in her heart was my life's obsession,
The love that I had for them would not
let me stay away.
So stripped of my powers I stand before you,
Just like you, yet still with envious stares,

Because you don't want my rehabilitation,
You're afraid of it,
For I am a formidable foe as a human,
And the most indomitable force as myself,
And knowing that the first step to recovery
Is acknowledging the problem,
I say to all of you,
Hi, My name is Superman, and I am addicted to Kryptonite.

THE ONE THAT GOT AWAY

YOU filled my void,
The sound of your voice
Calmed the raging seas in my mind
And gave me peace,
And a piece of me is willing to settle for
a piece of YOU,
But letting YOU leave seems like it would
leave me better off,
And if you'll be happy then I'll be okay,
I maintain that I would hate to see YOU leave,
But if you must go I wish YOU well,
I pray that YOU find the peace that YOU seek,
I hope that something can make YOU complete,
Though I would love for you to be content,
It's a sight that I would hate to see
If I had to watch YOU in love without me,
So I'll love YOU from afar,
I'll cherish YOU from a distance
And hope YOU never forget this love we had,
And maybe one day we can be friends,
But in the end YOU will always be
The one that got away.

THE GUARDIAN

I stand at the entrance
And I see your sign
"Under construction"
Hard hat on my head,
Toolbox in my hand,
Can we fix it?
Yes we can,
Yet you still tell me,
"I can't afford to hire a worker that will fail me",
In all your buildings frailty, I look to the foundation,
Now shaken by earthquakes and,
Compromised in its integrity,
Why? You said to me,
The workers before were of poor quality,
Cutting corners so they could get theirs and be out,
So now you work alone,
A young lady with nothing but some nails,
And a hammer, A screwdriver and a drill,
Still I feel you need me here,
So I leave my application,
And as you build, every time the walls crumble,
I'm outside waiting to rescue you,
And as I lift you from beneath the rubble,
You say I don't have to,
Because I don't work here,

But I still reach out and grab you,
Then I step back and watch you try to rebuild,
Ready to step in when you realize,
It's not your job alone,
Until that day I pray,
That when the walls crumble and fall,
I will always be an arm's length away,
To pull you to safety,
Love me or hate me,
I may not be the hero you want,
But I'm the hero you need.

THE MECHANIC

My greatest fear
Is to reach out for you
and nothing's there,
For you to disappear
Because our love has dissolved,
For you to walk away,
For you to say it's over,
For I've told you my deepest secrets,
I've given you the greatest pieces
Of my heart,
And I can't allow you to leave me here,
Because I've invested too much,
I'm interested too much
In the direction your life is heading,
And I can't see myself not being there,
Because I found you when you were broken,
I helped you pick up every fragment
Of your heart,
I even cut myself a few times in the process,
And I helped you put it all back together,
So you can never leave
And tell me that we'll never be,
Because I gave you everything,
I sacrificed all that I was
So that you could become all that you are

And you never could have come this far
Without me,
You are a masterpiece crafted by my hands,
And I refuse to see you in the arms of another man,
If you should decide to go,
I wish that I could wish you well,
But for the sake of self I wish you fail
And come running back to me,
So that I may have you for just a little longer
If only for repairs.

MASQUERADE

If it were not for the masquerade
Everyone would see the black parade
That is proceeding through your inner being,

But the disguise hides the eyes,
The pain and suffering
Become nothing but underlying themes

That nobody ever sees,
But sailing the seven seas
And seeing all the wonders of the world
Couldn't ease this pain,

Disheartened even at the sight of
Babylon's Hanging Gardens,
And the Colossus of Rhodes
Was nothing but a colossal disappointment,

So you join the masses,
Blending in with the throng
Pretending to be just what the
emotion on your mask is,
As you dance with the damsels

And partake in the festivities,
And the drinks at the bar
Make your memories elude you,
And the numbness temporarily soothes you,
You reach for another glass
And then your world begins to crash down

Like meteors to the Earth
Or like drunk drivers into the median,
As you seek to find some meaning in the room,
A purpose for your attendance at the soiree,
And you're just sorry that you can't enjoy the party,
But the mask traps your emotions beneath it

You bear a secret so heavy
That it may crush each and
Every one that you leak it to,
But it's eating you alive,
And if it weren't for the mask
Then they could see it in your eyes,
And you realize that solace may come too slowly,

But depression never takes it's time
in the minds of the lonely,
Your heart has been severed,
Your soul left derelict,
And in the end there was no one

to help with the mess
That she left when she left,

And no drug can alleviate the stress,
And you're just seeking to abbreviate
the pain if nothing else,
So you drown in the brown,
Find delight in the white,
And you hide under the covers
with different women every night,
And you still feel the same way
as the night before last
Every time you take off the mask.

KARMA'S HATE

The rivers that were cried for me lead into an endless ocean, but some say life's a vicious circle and an endless motion, but sometimes the go-round ain't so merry y'all, No lights it's very dark when life gets very hard,
When it seems like we gotta use rocks for pillows, And when it comes to weeping we don't stop like willows, Cuz my pain is all my fault,
To ex girl's I'm sorry for playin wit all y'all hearts, But I know too well that when Karma kicks in, Ain't no use for apologies cuz she not listenin', She just comin to avenge and give u what u earned, And hopefully u learned, but some still ain't concerned, And u keep doin wrong u don't think she comin back, Til u start havin nervous breakdowns can't keep yourself intact,
Now u start to get the picture but it's already too late, Cuz u fucked over one too many and you've earned Karma's hate, And you do everything just to earn Karma's smile, But no matter what you do, you won't see it for a while, Cuz all you sent around comes back around the course, Make sure you're careful on the carousel's high horse, And I learned the hard way that every heart you shatter, Karma uses every little piece as a dagger...

HYPOTHERMIA

I am the wise man amongst fools
And the fool amongst wise men,
The hero,
        the hated,
                the hypocrite
                        and the weak,
Yet you all believe I'm strong,
I am the whore of fate and destiny,
I am the blood of the innocent,
And the blade of the murderer,
I am everything to everybody,
Yet nothing to anybody,
The sole soul with the burden of carrying you
To a higher plane of existence,
I am torn down with the hope that
What remains will help to complete
your building process,
I am the broken record that plays the song
That I have written for you,
The beautiful ballad,
Once perfect,
                now skips and
                                becomes distorted,
My heart screams the screams of the tortured
At the painful stabs from the daggers you call words,

And as I lay in my broken dreams
and shattered hopes,
Black tears fall from my face
And become the ink to capture my soul's essence,
And as I express my love
You ignore the cries of my soul,
So I come to repossess my love
But the door you refuse to open,
So I wait in the blistering cold
And you never answer,
Taking my last phone calls
Sending my warm words of comfort
To those who "need" them
As emotional hypothermia sets in

BROKEN

Outside the stone fortress that was my heart,
I saw you standing, Your presence demanding
entrance, but I cannot let anyone in,
Yet, your powerful speeches moved me,
Your loving words touched me,
And you with your tenderness
Took me back to a place in which
Danger did not exist,
And I knew that I must let you in,
Yet this fortress that I had built
had no doors,
Only walls so high that no one
could ascend, So I tore down a
section of my wall, Just large
enough for you to slip through,
And as you entered,
I smiled a smile that I had not
smiled. Since the purity and
innocence of childhood, and ecstasy was seemingly
eternal, And then you reminded me why I built these
walls in the first place.

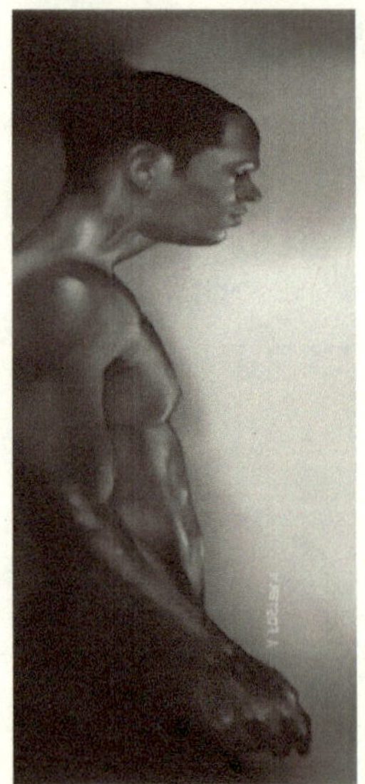

WANDERING ON

As he stands in the same place that she left him,
Seeming destined for this life of loneliness,
Only one thing keeping him in motion,
The notion that there is something
out there for everyone,
But what about the No One's?

As he reflected on her
And the new object of her affection
He recollected the moment
when he held that position,
Everything could have been so simple then,
But he was listening to his mind
And putting his heart on mute,
So the dispute that could have saved him
From feeling heart break
once again never transpired,
Ever sidling in and out of his mind
Was the thought that he would wander forever.

And though it was unsettling
Stressing held no benefits,
So he let go of all of his feelings,
Or so he thought,
Because he wanted so desperately

to mend his broken heart.

And so he walked,
Fancy free down the boulevard,
Greeting every stranger with a smile,
Gaining acquaintances for miles,
Who all called him friend.

But his presence was as ephemeral
As the silence between two notes in a song,
Before the first "I Love You's" were exchanged,
Nothing remained of him but his name.

Drifting from place to place,
Never letting the residents see his face,
Because the loneliness was far to somber
a sight to show
So wherever he chose to go
He decided that no one could know
Anything other than the mask.

The mask that held the smiles and hid the tears,
Camouflaged his fears with bravado,
Concealed the hollowness of his soul
By shielding his eyes from all those
Who would want to take a peek
through the spirit's window.

Because deep in the dark recesses of his mind
Hidden in the corner under some dreams
he had cast aside long ago
There lied the final piece of his fragile heart,
Delicate, but intact.
Precious, but untouched.
The only glimmer of hope,
The only sliver of consistency
In the life of a Wanderer.

THE DEBILITATION OF SUPERMAN

Whispers persist until they become screams in the dark, haunting me like fiends in the night. As I fiend and I fight for my independence from the stone that so deftly destroyed my world. Sleep has become fugitive to my body as I toss and I turn down every avenue to attempt to reach the street called Slumber. Nothing can give respite to my racing mind, and as paranoia sets in every drip from the faucet is like the gushing waters of Niagara Falls.

Every drop is like the waves crashing against the wall From the raging sea outside my window. Every creak is kryptonite creeping down the hall looking to leap back into my soul and return me to that living hell in which I once resided, but at least that Hell was a hell I knew. A hell I had been comfortable with, a hell that would be the same Hell every time I took a hit.

But now I just sit, sit in isolation, therapists telling me that deprivation is the key to my recovery, but can't they see me dying. Super Man isn't supposed to cry, but I wail to return to my own personal Hell, because even in daylight this darkness doesn't end.

Withdrawal sends my body into convulsions and causes expulsions of fluid from every orifice.

Once I stop shaking my muscles start aching and bouts of fever have me delusional. As the devil sits in the corner of my room engrossed in my destruction; Vigorous laughter echoing as he delights in my torment. I can't escape from this pain, emotionally and physically drained, as I scratch at the walls and scream for help. I am willing to take anything.

Inject me with something to stop this pain if only for a moment. My body rejects sobriety. How far I have fallen, a star from the heavens that has become just a mere rock on earth. As the nurses rush in with a drug that will restore my lucidity, I contemplate a way to break free, and I realize, the only way to get out of this hell, and back to my own, is to pretend to be okay. So I ignore the demons and I disregard the pain, and I feign recovery as I step through the threshold.

Out of their hell, and back to mine...

I WAS A KING

I was a King then
Flirting with immortality,
One step below the pantheon
Of the gods of this world,
I was the envy of all men,
The desire of all women,
But that was before the fall,
And just like the season
It brought about great change,
I saw the envious shades of green
Turn into shades of red that covered
Everything from shame to anger,
Stripped naked of my pride and my ego
Just as the trees are stripped of their leaves,
Paraded in front of my former
kingdom as a mere mortal,
And locked away as a common criminal,
As the Queen that had manipulated me so
Sat and watched with a look of indifference,
Apathetic to my fate,
For as long as I was locked away
She could rule forever,
So I vowed to destroy her
by any means necessary,
If the destruction of self,

meant the destruction of the Queen,
Then destruction of self was imminent,
Being forced to agree to live as a peasant
In my own kingdom,
I was freed,
I walked the same streets
as my old mistresses,
Women I had tossed aside like rag dolls,
Women that jeered and even cheered at my demise,
I worked alongside the men,
Men that I had robbed of their lovers,
Fathers of daughters whose lives I had destroyed,
But I had no shame, I held no sympathy,
But I feigned remorse, of course,
For no purpose other than to remain safe,
And with each passing day,
the people grew more cordial,
The constituents of the land began to rediscover
the love they once had
For a man that was once a King,
And at that moment,
An idea hit me like a ton of bricks,
Insurrection, if I could just plant the seeds of
rebellion against the Queen,
I could reclaim my throne,
So I released the idea of insurgence

like a whisper in the wind,
And every townsperson began to grow restless,
Every man, woman, and child
desired a change of regime,
And who better to lead than a fallen King,
As we converged upon the castle,
We set fire to the fields outside it,
We ravaged the gardens within the castle walls,
We plundered the buildings of the nobility,
Casualties amassed quickly on both sides,
As even I felt the cold steel pierce my skin,
But we continued to fight valiantly,
And as I forced my way into the library,
There she stood,
That wretched Queen with her eyes fixated on the books that held my secrets,
Her eyes been to glaze over as if she knew these were her last moments on Earth,
As my sword was stained with the blood of her knights and my eyes were seething with anger,
But as I moved toward her
My heart began to soften
And my resolve began to fade,
And I dropped my sword and held her in my arms,
And as we kissed our final kiss,
She whispered "I love you",
Those same three words that had set my world ablaze so long ago spared her life, for I could not

turn her over to the peasants,
So I exiled her never to return again,
And once more, I was a King then,
Flirting with immortality, one step below the pantheon Of the gods of this world.

THE RISE

THE RELAPSE OF SUPERMAN

Deception shall set you free, for if I had told the truth I'd still be fighting tooth and nail, attempting to break free from that indelible hell. Instead, I walked right through the door unimpeded; only slowed by congratulations. If they only knew, as soon as I stepped out of that infernal building I would go right back to the Heavenly Hell that was my Kryptonite-induced high.

Surprisingly enough, my dealer was not the first thing I sought. Proper rest and nourishment was necessary for my body to survive this next hit,
I was finally able to eat and sleep peacefully knowing that I was free to use anytime I pleased,
And as my days got busier, my desire weakened. Kryptonite becoming a mere afterthought; Super Man was back after being out of commission for so long.

The world was in more turmoil than ever, left without a hero, and with every person I saved
I felt my strength beginning to return. As I once again began to transcend my contemporaries and ascend unto the skies, and that natural high that I had long ago forgotten was enough to make me forget about Kryptonite.

I heard the cries of despair from afar, a familiar voice that I could not pinpoint. A despondent cry that beckoned for a hero, as I raced to the scene I couldn't help but think about where I knew that voice, racking my brain for answers, but before a solution came to mind I had reached my location. As I defeated the villains, I felt my powers begin to dissipate, and before I even approached the victim I knew who she was, a grim reality stared me in the face. As she gazed into my eyes and smiled that helpless smile, and I saw that stone, glowing red, Calling me to take one more hit.

SKY BLUES

It's hard keeping faith
When your enemies
seem like they have
a stronghold on your fate,
When your love walks away,
No food on your plate,
When she's taking you for granted,
When you're losing all the
people you called family,
And you're going half insane
Because it's hard to ascertain
Whether it's real what she's sayin,
Or is she just running game,
And you love her
But these women keep coming,
And you appreciate the love,
But that's your woman,
And nothing can take her place,
Plus people you used to call friends
Only stare you in the face
When you walk by,
And you're trying to see further
like a hawk eye,
But your vision is blurred,
The situation that has occurred

Is an amazing disaster,
It's crazy and absurd,
And for the first time in years,
Your words mean nothing here,
Mostly because nobody wants to lend an ear,
Swallowing tears, obstructing your windpipe,
Trying to keep your head up, Enzyte,
You still fight when your back's against the wall,
Everything's all against you
and they're stacking up the odds,
And you were flying too high,
Cause a flood if you cry,
If you fell you would die,
Your only choice is to hide behind the sky...

INSUFFICIENT

I'm a little bit rude, a little uncool,
And a little unsmooth for a woman like you,
Weird in my ways, nothing like the rest,
I am so much more to you, but so much less,
Cuz though I'm the best, I guess I'm the worst,
Yes, I'm blessed with a curse,
To love til it hurts, To give til it's gone,
To still treat you right
even when you treat me wrong,
Chasing love as I watch you escape to the horizons,
Waiting on a time when, I can come and fly with,
You, But I move with broken wings,
You seem like another disappointment in my life full
of broken dreams,
So I'm focusing,
Doors closing but I'm looking for the opening,
Wishing you would notice me,
But you're gonna leave me
standing out in the cold it seems,
The world is much colder with no one to hold ya,
No jacket to warm ya, No fleece pullovers,
But in the end, remember what I told ya,
I love you like a nun loves Jehovah

IRREPLACEABLE

If you're expecting me to let you leave
Without any attempt to stop you
You've got me all wrong,
We've got things to talk about,
So tell me what you're talking about,
What do you mean you're walking out
And going back to your mommas house,
We've both made mistakes,
But by no means
Should we let faux pas turn into au revoir,
For we've traveled too far on this journey,
Too many arguments that should be trumped
By too much fun,
Too many tears and too many screams
That should be shaded by the laughs we had,
Too many opinions voiced from the outside,
Too much finger pointing and not enough
accountability,
So I will no longer play the blame game
Because at the end of the day
I'll say whatever I have to say
To make you stay,
I'll absolve you from all guilt
If it will solve all our problems,
I'll admit that it's all been my fault,

Because I forgot that you were a Queen
And I forgot to do the things that brought you here,
Amnesia setting in at the most inappropriate times,
Forgetting to compliment you on your new hairstyle,
And taking your extraordinary smile for granted
Just because I saw it ordinarily,
And I'll concede that I'm not the man I was
When you thought that you would marry me,
But one thing that has not changed
Is my desire for the better half of me to live happily,
Even if it means I have to let you go,
But I just wanna let you know
That I will always be here
Should you decide to return,
And I know that I left a stain
but I resolve to clean any mess I made,
And yes I pray that God restores my blessing
That I neglected and ran ragged,
And I hope that He and I can work together
To restore your faith in me,
And I know hating me is easy now,
But I'm begging you don't leave me now
Or just don't leave me out in the cold alone,
Because what was once a perfect home
Has turned into another sad song,
A song without words,
Just a few notes in the key of despair,
And I'm not keeping you here against your will,

But I'll give you the key to my heart,
And you never have to use it,
I just ask you never lose it in case
You decide to return,
But maybe if you double back,
The love we used to have
We can work to double that
And soar to heights that we never before imagined,
So I speak this phrase "I love you"
And hope it's not the last one
That we exchange because the
fact remains that you are
Irreplaceable.

A STEP BACK

If we could,
Take just a moment
To step away from the crowd,
Settle down and gather our thoughts,
Then maybe we could talk
And possibly get a few things accomplished,
If we could,
Stop publicizing our relationship like open mic
Maybe we could escape the hatred
Of our friends and foes alike,
Because your friends
Begin to enter in your presence
Bearing bad news
About someone new they saw me with,
And how I'd forgotten you,
And my friends all seem to have the inside scoop
About who's trying to taste your 31 flavors,
And all it does is escalate the tension,
Attention focused on everything
Except the matter at hand,
Which happens to be
How do we make reparations
To our current situation,
Placing emphasis on the love,
Because obviously we forgot

What got us here,
We were younger then,
We were inseparable,
The love was unspoken but the trust was unbroken,
And we were never open to
the thought of leaving each other,
But now we beef with each other
Because love was not enough to override mistrust,
They say love is nothing without trust,
So was it lust,
Or was it just an act
Once the lies set foot in the door,
And we're just trying to make it back to the love
But there's no map to the love,
It takes a lot of hard work and practice for love,
And I was being Allen Iverson,
"Practice? Why we talking' bout practice"
When the fact is that was all that mattered,
Was putting in the work
And getting down the fundamentals,
So as we attempt to get back to the basics,
We're gonna need some separation,
Not from each other,
But from the crowd

WAR OF OUR WORLDS

As our two worlds collide,
God has written a message in the stars,
Rather, Painted a picture,
Not of our worlds struggling for supremacy,
Mine to rule, Yours to remain Independent,
But for our two worlds to coalesce,
Into a powerful entity that can conquer anything,
And everything, You are my everything,
And I'd do anything,
To bring into fruition the
constellation that is you and me,
I hear a voice that says all in time,
So I search for a catalyst to speed up the process,
Or at least to see the result,
Because surely, If our worlds cannot merge,
Mine faces obsoleteness, and maybe even obliteration,
A war of the worlds that I cannot lose,
Because in this war,
The aim is peace, Love and happiness,
For both worlds, Harmony is the key to survival,
Yet only the musicians of your world
hold the instruments That can play the notes
That populate my symphony, So Love, Look to the
stars,
And fulfill their wishes.

BIRTH BY FLAME

As the world burns around us
And debris rains from the sky,
I remember when we
reigned
over
all
of
this
So I guess it's true that it all falls down,
But when you're at the top
You forget about the ground
And how it feels to land,
I expected you to flee
When the walls were breached
And started to crumble,
As the earth started to rumble
From the footsteps of destruction, but
here
we
stand,
Hand
in
hand,
Baptized in ashes, preparing to rise again
Through the flames

12-21-2012

Slowly, we are growing closer
Taking the pace we're supposed to,
And yet it's not enough,
Since all we have is time I suppose
That we don't wanna rush,
We keep it hushed and let the
public perception be what it may
And still a little tense when we lay,
Afraid to fall any deeper into
each
others
arms,
Afraid to look any deeper into
each
others
eyes,
All because we have nothing but time,
And I don't believe the Mayans
But right about now
I am thinking that
we should love like it's
12-21-2012,

Love like there will never
be
another
second,

Love like you will never
see
anyone
else,

It's **12-21-2012,**

And there will never be another moment like this,
There will never be another moment,
So let's love with all the love we can find within
Before it ends,
And maybe it won't but only time will tell,
But until then,
love me
Like it's **12-21-2012**

LIBERATION

Let me liberate you,
Come with me and learn to be free,
Release your inhibitions
And throw caution to the wind,
If only for one night,
Let me reiterate
That I'm just trying to liberate you,
I'm just trying to take you
To a place called ecstasy,
Where hedonism is the religion
And gratification is the reward,
Where egos run low and sensuality runs high,
Where pride is pushed aside
For the purpose of satisfaction,
Where the only pain is pleasure,
And the only thing between us
Is the sweat that drips from our intertwined bodies,
This is the embodiment of sexuality,
Look up in the sky
And see the astral projections
Of our bodies in the constellations,
As our spirits lift into the heavens,
Higher and higher,
Contentment sending the very essence of our being
Into a state of constant ascension,

Free from the pressures of the world,
Free from the societal norms that
say what we do is taboo,
Emancipated from personal reservations,
Though you reserve the right
To walk right back into your quiet life,
And jump back in your box,
I implore you to stay and enjoy
Liberation

FANTASIES

I could tell you all the things I want to do to you,
But where's the fun in that,
As my hands slowly run down your back
And make your spine tingle
You react with a shudder,
You've never felt another touch like this,
As I lean over and kiss your neck
I see you begin to melt,
As you close your eyes
And let your mind travel to a supernatural
Plane of existence,
Because you are no longer Plain Jane,
You are an empress,
You are a goddess,
And I am but a servant of pleasure,
My next move will be directly from your fantasy,
Playing out a scene straight out of a dream,
What is your command,
Just make sure you can handle it,
My hands can do magic tricks
That make you forget who you are,
And if I go any farther
You may get caught up in the rapture, Miss,
and I will never miss the spot,
I'll get you hotter than high noon in the desert,

But I'm cooler than an Arabian night,
Maybe I might throw in a trick or two
That may leave you addicted to what I do,
Or you could show me your moves,
And I could do the same things you're used to,
But ain't no pleasure like new pleasure,
So I'll do whatever you've yet to try,
I'll be the artist that paints your concepts,
And you can be my muse,
But you must tell me what to do,
For I don't have fantasies,
I just fulfill them.

EXCEPTIONAL

Infatuated by an exceptional you
From the way that you move,
To your ambition,
To the sexual you,
From the texture of your hair
To the clarity of your skin,
From your angel eyes
To your devilish grin,
You are exceptional,
And to get to know you
Any better would be to fall in love
And I'm just not ready,
But everything you do brings me ever closer
To wanting to stay and forever hold you,
Exceptional in everything you do,
Humility with an attitude,
Conservative eccentricity,
Natural hair and earth tones
In tune with your ethnicity,
With the finest designer perfumes,
Exceptionally fragranced,
Flagrantly aromatic,
Blatantly sexy,
Exceptionally so,

And you run the show
And somehow still let me show you the way,
And the way you dominate me
Through your submissiveness
I must admit it is exceptional,
The way you exude eroticism
In the simplest of tasks
Makes me bask in the fact
That my woman is exceptional,
And if I lost it all except for you,
It wouldn't matter
Because you are
phenomenal,
Astounding,
One
of
a
kind,
Exceptional

NEW QUEEN

As I look upon a land, once great,
Now barren and desolate,
I bow to show reverence to its
past leaders and residents,
The different regions and settlements
of former queens,
The palaces of shattered hopes and torn up dreams,
The various memories of the heart attacks,
The images of the invaders and
even some of their artifacts,
The advent of love, and also the destruction,
All of the corruption caused by the queens' injustice,
A wasteland once filled with happiness
now shrouded in the midst
Of hatred and misery, bliss doesn't exist,
Looking over the ruins preparing for restoration,
Rebuilding an empire, spirits are elevating,
Searching for a new queen,
But this will never again happen,
So to make sure she can't corrupt me,
make her monarchy democratic,
This is MY land, and I stand sovereign,
And I will make sure from now on
my queen's love isn't counterfeit,
And even if it is

She will never have the power
To destroy my radiant gardens,
I'll build a fortress around my flowers,
Seek respite in my sanctuary,
My inner sanctum,
Way beneath the main entrance,
deep in the inner chamber,
No access for any other soul,
Just me, and me only,
And I'll resurface to my queen
whenever I feel lonely...

FINAL DESTINATION

As the Wanderer picked up his hat
To continue upon his quest for stability,
He paused, just for a moment
To reflect on all of the places he had been.

And there was no denying
That though he had seen many sights,
The feeling of emptiness that plagued his soul
Had taken hold of him.

There was no risk involved if no one knew his heart,
But there was also no reward to come,
And his heart might survive
But never be utilized because he never knew love.

He became cognizant of the fact
That his nomadic lifestyle could only
lead to loneliness,
A fate worse than death,
Never to love or be loved in return.

He began to rationalize
As he journeyed toward the next town,
What if I give love and don't get it back,
For no love is worse than a love unrequited.

As he trudged along his path
A figure approached him,
His eyes were transfixed on the
curvature of her silhouette,
His mind was blown by the grace that she embodied.

In that instance he made up his mind
to alter his fate,
He bumped into her seemingly by accident,
Helping her gather her things
Which he noticed were few in number.

He asked where she was going,
She replied, "Nowhere",
He asked where she came from,
And she replied, "Nowhere."

His eyes were immediately filled with jubilation,
As he came to the understanding
That she, just like him,
Was a Wanderer.

With all of his inhibitions beginning to fade,
He removed his mask and gazed into her eyes,
He glared into her very being
To find a girl just as helpless as he was.

And neither of them judged
For they both held dark pasts,
Rather, they embraced the idea
Of having a comrade.

As he took hold of her hand,
He said these words,
"I don't know where we came from,
And I don't know where we're going,
But if we must walk aimlessly,
Let us wander under the guidance of Love."

Superman is Alive

Right back in the mix, I know you missed me right? I've been busy kicking my addiction to the Kryptonite. Rehabilitated and Reinvigorated, I'm looking at you haters got you sick a brother made it. Had a couple rough spots thought they was messing up the painting, but it all falls in place, Life's a bigger picture ain't it, Swagger back intact, Feelings back in place, Working at full strength, running at full pace, Catch me if you can, Mr. Leonardo,
If yesterday was sorrow, just look forward to tomorrow,
Just a conqueror of things,
That to many folks would seem
Like insurmountable tasks,
But they're peasants I'm a king,
To your women I'm a dream,
Wishing they could get with him,
Spit to them so similar in synonyms,
Killing them softly with a song so sweet,
Only one can make me fly down and sweep her off her feet, My new mindset is forget it, If you don't want a savior, the first time I come then don't call me back to save you, Superman is back, Like he never left, Ready for whatever and whatever else.

~Ghost

www.ingramcontent.com/pod-product-compliance
Lightning Source LLC
LaVergne TN
LVHW091011080826
845145LV00003B/1228

* 9 7 8 0 9 8 2 6 7 4 5 7 4 *